SLAUGHTERHOUSE-FIVE

Kurt Vonnegut

© 2002 by Spark Publishing

SPARKNOTES is a registered trademark of SparkNotes LLC

Spark Publishing
A Division of Barnes & Noble
120 Fifth Avenue
New York, NY 10011
www.sparknotes.com

ISBN-13: 978-1-5866-3458-2
ISBN-10: 1-5866-3458-5

Please submit changes or report errors to www.sparknotes.com/errors.

Printed and bound in the United States.

20 19 18 17 16 15 14 13 12 11

INTRODUCTION:
STOPPING TO BUY SPARKNOTES ON A SNOWY EVENING

Whose words these are you *think* you know.
Your paper's due tomorrow, though;
We're glad to see you stopping here
To get some help before you go.

Lost your course? You'll find it here.
Face tests and essays without fear.
Between the words, good grades at stake:
Get great results throughout the year.

Once school bells caused your heart to quake
As teachers circled each mistake.
Use SparkNotes and no longer weep,
Ace every single test you take.

Yes, books are lovely, dark, and deep,
But only what you grasp you keep,
With hours to go before you sleep,
With hours to go before you sleep.

CONTENTS

CONTEXT

K URT VONNEGUT, JR. WAS BORN in Indianapolis in 1922, a descendant of prominent German-American families. His father was an architect and his mother was a noted beauty. Both spoke German fluently but declined to teach Kurt the language in light of widespread anti-German sentiment following World War I. Family money helped send Vonnegut's two siblings to private schools. The Great Depression hit hard in the 1930s, though, and the family placed Kurt in public school while it moved to more modest accommodations. While in high school, Vonnegut edited the school's daily newspaper. He attended college at Cornell for a little over two years, with instructions from his father and brother to study chemistry, a subject at which he did not excel. He also wrote for the *Cornell Daily Sun*. In 1943 he enlisted in the U.S. Army. In 1944 his mother committed suicide, and Vonnegut was taken prisoner following the Battle of the Bulge, in the Ardennes Forest of Belgium.

After the war, Vonnegut married and entered a master's degree program in anthropology at the University of Chicago. He also worked as a reporter for the Chicago City News Bureau. His master's thesis, titled *Fluctuations Between Good and Evil in Simple Tales*, was rejected. He departed for Schenectady, New York, to take a job in public relations at a General Electric research laboratory.

Vonnegut left GE in 1951 to devote himself full-time to writing. During the 1950s, Vonnegut published short stories in national magazines. *Player Piano*, his first novel, appeared in 1952. *Sirens of Titan* was published in 1959, followed by *Mother Night* (1962), *Cat's Cradle* (1963), *God Bless You, Mr. Rosewater* (1965), and his most highly praised work, *Slaughterhouse-Five* (1969). Vonnegut continues to write prolifically.

Slaughterhouse-Five treats one of the most horrific massacres in European history—the World War II firebombing of Dresden, a city in eastern Germany, on February 13, 1945—with mock-serious humor and clear antiwar sentiment. More than 130,000 civilians died in Dresden, roughly the same number of deaths that resulted from the Allied bombing raids on Tokyo and from the atomic bomb dropped on Hiroshima, both of which also occurred in 1945. Inhabitants of Dresden were incinerated or suffocated in a matter of hours as a firestorm sucked up and consumed available oxygen. The scene on the ground was one of unimaginable destruction.

The novel is based on Kurt Vonnegut's own experience in World War II. In the novel, a prisoner of war witnesses and survives the Allied forces' firebombing of Dresden. Vonnegut, like his protagonist Billy Pilgrim, emerged from a meat locker beneath a slaughterhouse into the moonscape of burned-out Dresden. His surviving captors put him to work finding, burying, and burning bodies. His task continued until the Russians came and the war ended. Vonnegut survived by chance, confined as a prisoner of war (POW) in a well-insulated meat locker, and so missed the cataclysmic moment of attack, emerging the day after into the charred ruins of a once-beautiful cityscape. Vonnegut has said that he always intended to write about the experience but found himself incapable of doing so for more than twenty years. Although he attempted to describe in simple terms what happened and to create a linear narrative, this strategy never worked for him. Billy Pilgrim's unhinged time—shifting, a mechanism for dealing with the unfathomable aggression and mass destruction he witnesses, is Vonnegut's solution to the problem of telling an untellable tale.

Vonnegut wrote *Slaughterhouse-Five* as a response to war. "It is so short and jumbled and jangled," he explains in Chapter 1, "because there is nothing intelligent to say about a massacre." The jumbled structure of the novel and the long delay between its conception and completion serve as testaments to a very personal struggle with heart-wrenching material. But the timing of the novel's publication also deserves notice: in 1969, the United States was in the midst of the dismal Vietnam War. Vonnegut was an outspoken pacifist and critic of the conflict. *Slaughterhouse-Five* revolves around the willful incineration of 100,000 civilians, in a city of extremely dubious military significance, during an arguably just war. Appearing when it did, then, *Slaughterhouse-Five* made a forceful statement about the campaign in Vietnam, a war in which incendiary technology was once more being employed against non-military targets in the name of a dubious cause.

PLOT OVERVIEW

NOTE: *Billy Pilgrim, the novel's protagonist, has become "unstuck in time." He travels between periods of his life, unable to control which period he lands in. As a result, the narrative is not chronological or linear. Instead, it jumps back and forth in time and place. The novel is structured in small sections, each several paragraphs long, that describe various moments of his life.*

Billy Pilgrim is born in 1922 and grows up in Ilium, New York. A funny-looking, weak youth, he does reasonably well in high school, enrolls in night classes at the Ilium School of Optometry, and is drafted into the army during World War II. He trains as a chaplain's assistant in South Carolina, where an umpire officiates during practice battles and announces who survives and who dies before they all sit down to lunch together. Billy's father dies in a hunting accident shortly before Billy ships overseas to join an infantry regiment in Luxembourg. Billy is thrown into the Battle of the Bulge in Belgium and is immediately taken prisoner behind German lines. Just before his capture, he experiences his first incident of time—shifting: he sees the entirety of his life, from beginning to end, in one sweep.

Billy is transported in a crowded railway boxcar to a POW camp in Germany. Upon his arrival, he and the other privates are treated to a feast by a group of fellow prisoners, who are English officers who were captured earlier in the war. Billy suffers a breakdown and gets a shot of morphine that sends him time-tripping again. Soon he and the other Americans travel onward to the beautiful city of Dresden, still relatively untouched by wartime privation. Here the prisoners must work for their keep at various labors, including the manufacture of a nutritional malt syrup. Their camp occupies a former slaughterhouse. One night, Allied forces carpet bomb the city, then drop incendiary bombs to create a firestorm that sucks most of the oxygen into the blaze, asphyxiating or incinerating roughly 130,000 people. Billy and his fellow POWs survive in an airtight meat locker. They emerge to find a moonscape of destruction, where they are forced to excavate corpses from the rubble. Several days later, Russian forces capture the city, and Billy's involvement in the war ends.

Billy returns to Ilium and finishes optometry school. He gets engaged to Valencia Merble, the obese daughter of the school's founder. After a nervous breakdown, Billy commits himself to a veterans' hospital and receives shock treatments. During his stay in the mental ward, a fellow patient introduces Billy to the science fiction novels of a writer named Kilgore Trout. After his recuperation, Billy gets married. His wealthy father-in-law sets him up in the optometry business, and Billy and Valencia raise two children and grow rich. Billy acquires the trappings of the suburban American dream: a Cadillac, a stately home with modern appliances, a bejeweled wife, and the presidency of the Lions Club. He is not aware of keeping any secrets from himself, but at his eighteenth wedding anniversary party the sight of a barbershop quartet makes him break down because, he realizes, it triggers a memory of Dresden.

The night after his daughter's wedding in 1967, as he later reveals on a radio talk show, Billy is kidnapped by two-foot-high aliens who resemble upside-down toilet plungers, who he says are called Tralfamadorians. They take him in their flying saucer to the planet Tralfamadore, where they mate him with a movie actress named Montana Wildhack. She, like Billy, has been brought from Earth to live under a transparent geodesic dome in a zoo where Tralfamadorians can observe extraterrestrial curiosities. The Tralfamadorians explain to Billy their perception of time, how its entire sweep exists for them simultaneously in the fourth dimension. When someone dies, that person is simply dead at a particular time. Somewhere else and at a different time he or she is alive and well. Tralfamadorians prefer to look at life's nicer moments.

When he returns to Earth, Billy initially says nothing of his experiences. In 1968, he gets on a chartered plane to go to an optometry conference in Montreal. The plane crashes into a mountain, and, among the optometrists, only Billy survives. A brain surgeon operates on him in a Vermont hospital. On her way to visit him there, Valencia dies of accidental carbon monoxide poisoning after crashing her car. Billy's daughter places him under the care of a nurse back home in Ilium. But he feels that the time is ripe to tell the world what he has learned. Billy has foreseen this moment while time-tripping, and he knows that his message will eventually be accepted. He sneaks off to New York City, where he goes on a radio talk show. Shortly thereafter, he writes a letter to the local paper. His daughter is at her wit's end and does not know what to do with him. Billy makes a tape recording of his account of his death, which he predicts will occur in 1976 after Chicago has been hydrogen-bombed by the Chinese. He knows exactly how it will happen: a vengeful man he knew in the war will hire someone to shoot him. Billy adds that he will experience the violet hum of death and then will skip back to some other point in his life. He has seen it all many times.

CHARACTER LIST

Billy Pilgrim A World War II veteran, POW survivor of the firebombing of Dresden, prospering optometrist, husband, and father. Billy Pilgrim is the protagonist of the novel who believes he has "come unstuck in time." He walks through a door at one moment in his life and suddenly finds himself in another time and place. His fragmented experience of time structures the novel as short episodic vignettes and shows how the difficulty of recounting traumatic experiences can require unusual literary techniques.

Kurt Vonnegut The novel's author and a minor character. Vonnegut himself was a prisoner of war during the firebombing of Dresden, and he periodically inserts himself in the narrative, as when he becomes the incontinent soldier in the latrine in the German prison camp. This authorial presence reappears throughout the novel, particularly in the refrain "So it goes" that follows each mention of death. Vonnegut's commentary as a character and an author enables a more factual interpretation of a story that seems almost preternaturally fictional and adds support to the idea that such fantastical elements may be the reality of a traumatized mind.

Bernhard V. O'Hare A wartime pal of Vonnegut. O'Hare appears when Vonnegut visits him and his wife in Pennsylvania while trying to do research and collect remembrances for his Dresden book. Like his wife, Mary, and Vonnegut himself, O'Hare, a nonfictional character, helps ground *Slaughterhouse-Five* in reality. Vonnegut actually has this other survivor of the firebombing contribute to the research and recollection process involved in creating the book, which allows us to take the novelistic details as fact and appreciate the thoughtful manner in which they are presented.

Mary O'Hare Bernhard O'Hare's wife. Mary gets upset with Vonnegut because she believes that he will glorify war in his novel; Vonnegut, however, promises not to do so. *Slaughterhouse-Five* is a condemnation of war, and Vonnegut's decision to dedicate the novel in part to Mary suggests how deeply he agrees with her that the ugly truth about war must be told.

Gerhard Müller The nonfictional taxi driver who takes Vonnegut and O'Hare back to their Dresden slaughterhouse. Müller later sends O'Hare a Christmas card bearing tidings of peace, and Vonnegut dedicates the novel in part to Müller—two simple gestures of sympathy that stand out amid the novel's pervasive cruelty and violence.

Roland Weary A stupid, cruel soldier taken prisoner by the Germans along with Billy. Unlike Billy, who is totally out of place in the war, Weary is a deluded glory-seeker who fancies himself part of the Three Musketeers and saves Billy's life out of a desire to be heroic.

Wild Bob An army colonel in the German rail yard who has lost his mind. Wild Bob asks if Billy belongs to his regiment when, in fact, all his men are dead. He invites everyone to visit him in Wyoming, but his arbitrary death shows how the war makes such gestures both poignant and pointless.

Paul Lazzaro Another POW and the man responsible for Billy's death. Lazzaro, a revenge-loving ruffian with criminal tendencies, arranges for Billy's assassination to avenge Roland Weary's death. Lazzaro's determination to kill Billy does not create a conflict between the two characters, however; because Billy has accepted the Tralfamadorians' conception of nonlinear time, he is unconcerned by his death.

Edgar Derby Another survivor of Dresden's incineration.
Following the firebombing, Derby is sentenced to die
by firing squad for plundering a teapot from the
wreckage. His death is anticlimactic, since Billy does
not view it with any sense of pathos, but rather as
an inevitability.

Valencia Merble Billy's pleasant, fat wife who loves him dearly.
Valencia and Billy share a well-appointed home and
have two children together, but Billy consistently
distances himself from his family.

Tralfamadorians Aliens shaped like toilet plungers, each with
one hand containing an eye in its palm. The
Tralfamadorians' philosophies of time and death
influence the narrative style of the novel. They perceive
time as an assemblage of moments existing
simultaneously rather than as a linear progression, and
the episodic nature of *Slaughterhouse-Five* reflects this
notion of time. Their acceptance of death, which Billy
embraces, leads the narrator to remark simply "So it
goes" at each mention of death.

Eliot Rosewater A war veteran who occupies the bed near Billy
in the mental ward of a veterans' hospital. Like Billy,
Rosewater is suffering from the aftereffects of war, and
he finds escape—and helps Billy find escape—in the
science-fiction novels of Kilgore Trout.

Kilgore Trout A bitter, unappreciated author of several cleverly
ironic science-fiction novels that have a great influence
on Billy. Trout, who appears in many of Vonnegut's
works, functions as Vonnegut's alter ego.

Howard W. Campbell, Jr. An American who has become a
Nazi. Campbell speaks to the prisoners in the
slaughterhouse and tries to recruit them for "The Free
American Corps," a German army unit that he is
forming to fight the Russians. Campbell represents all
that is wrong with war; he desires to use people for
perverse ideological ends.

Werner Gluck A young German guard at the slaughterhouse. Gluck gets his first glimpse of a naked woman along with Billy. Their shared intrigue and interest in the naked female body unites these two men from different sides, reflecting how fundamentally human feelings—such as lust—can trump differences of political ideology.

Montana Wildhack A nubile young actress who is kidnapped by the Tralfamadorians to be Billy's mate inside the zoo. Billy wins Montana's trust and love, and fathers a child by her in Tralfamadore. But Billy likely is delusional about his experiences with Montana, whose presence may have been imaginatively triggered by a visit to an adult bookstore in Times Square, where he sees her videos and a headline claiming to reveal her fate.

Barbara Pilgrim Billy's daughter, newly married at the age of twenty-one, who is faced with the sudden death of her mother and the apparent mental breakdown of her father. Barbara represents the follow-up generation to the one ravaged by World War II. While Billy's ability to function in life and be successful in a career paves the way for Barbara's development, his war trauma and delusions constantly frustrate her.

Bertram Copeland Rumfoord A Harvard history professor and the official U.S. Air Force historian who is laid up by a skiing accident in the same Vermont hospital as Billy after his plane crash. Rumfoord's reluctance to believe that Billy was present during the Dresden raid embodies the bureaucratic attitude that seeks to glorify the war and its heroes instead of realistically portraying war's destructiveness and its haphazard selection of survivors.

Lily Rumfoord Rumfoord's young trophy wife and research assistant. Lily Rumfoord is frightened of Billy, but she lies silent in the next bed as a symbol of the scope of powerlessness and lack of free will.

Robert Pilgrim Billy's son, who is a failure and a delinquent at school, though he cleans up his life enough to become a Green Beret in the Vietnam War. Robert's presence in the story during Billy's later life helps illustrate the pervasiveness of Billy's war trauma, especially his inability to communicate and relate to his own son. Robert's successful self-reformation from delinquency to discipline (in Vietnam) seems to indicate Vonnegut's acceptance of the inevitability of war.

Billy's mother Billy's mother is described as a woman "trying to construct a life that made sense from things she found in gift shops" (she once hung a grisly crucifix in Billy's room but never joined a church because she couldn't settle on a denomination). She visits Billy in the mental hospital, and her presence embarrasses him because he feels like an ungrateful son for being indifferent to life.

Billy's father Billy's father throws young Billy into the YMCA pool to teach him how to swim. Billy prefers the bottom of the pool, but he is rescued unwillingly from drowning after he loses consciousness. This incident initiates the novel's theme of the illusory nature of free will.

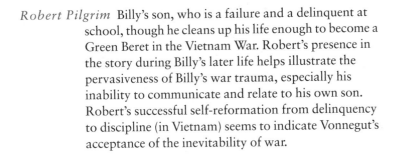

CHARACTER LIST

CHARACTER ANALYSIS

BILLY PILGRIM

Billy Pilgrim is the unlikeliest of antiwar heroes. An unpopular and complacent weakling even before the war (he prefers sinking to swimming), he becomes a joke as a soldier. He trains as a chaplain's assistant, a duty that earns him disgust from his peers. With scant preparation for armed conflict, no weapons, and even an improper uniform, he is thrust abruptly into duty at the Battle of the Bulge. The farcical spectacle created by Billy's inappropriate clothing accentuates the absurdity of such a scrawny, mild-mannered soldier. His azure toga, a leftover scrap of stage curtain, and his fur-lined overcoat, several sizes too small, throw his incongruity into relief. They underscore a central irony: such a creature could walk through war, oblivious yet unscathed, while so many others with more appropriate attire and provisions perish. It is in this shocked and physically exhausted state that Billy first comes "unstuck in time" and begins swinging to and fro through the events of his life, past and future.

Billy lives a life full of indignity and so, perhaps, has no great fear of death. He is oddly suited, therefore, to the Tralfamadorian philosophy of accepting death. This fact may point to an interpretation of the Tralfamadorians as a figment of Billy's disturbed mind, an elaborate coping mechanism to explain the meaningless slaughter Billy has witnessed. By uttering "So it goes" after each death, the narrator, like Billy, does not diminish the gravity of death but rather lends an equalizing dignity to all death, no matter how random or ironic, how immediate or removed. Billy's father dies in a hunting accident just as Billy is about to go off to war. So it goes. A former hobo dies in Billy's railway car while declaring the conditions not bad at all. So it goes. One hundred thirty thousand innocent people die in Dresden. So it goes. Valencia Pilgrim accidentally kills herself with carbon monoxide after turning bright blue. So it goes. Billy Pilgrim is killed by an assassin's bullet at exactly the time he has predicted, in the realization of a thirty-some-year-old death threat. So it goes. Billy awaits death calmly, without fear, knowing the exact hour at which it will come. In so doing, he gains a degree of control over his own dignity that he has lacked throughout most of his life.

The novel centers on Billy Pilgrim to a degree that excludes the development of the supporting characters, who exist in the text only as they relate to Billy's experience of events.

THEMES, MOTIFS & SYMBOLS

THEMES

Themes are the fundamental and often universal ideas explored in a literary work.

THE DESTRUCTIVENESS OF WAR

Whether we read *Slaughterhouse-Five* as a science-fiction novel or a quasi-autobiographical moral statement, we cannot ignore the destructive properties of war, since the catastrophic firebombing of the German town of Dresden during World War II situates all of the other seemingly random events. From his swimming lessons at the YMCA to his speeches at the Lions Club to his captivity in Tralfamadore, Billy Pilgrim shifts in and out of the meat locker in Dresden, where he very narrowly survives asphyxiation and incineration in a city where fire is raining from the sky.

However, the not-so-subtle destructiveness of the war is evoked in subtle ways. For instance, Billy is quite successful in his postwar exploits from a materialistic point of view: he is president of the Lions Club, works as a prosperous optometrist, lives in a thoroughly comfortable modern home, and has fathered two children. While Billy seems to have led a productive postwar life, these seeming markers of success speak only to its surface. He gets his job not because of any particular prowess but as a result of his father-in-law's efforts. More important, at one point in the novel, Billy walks in on his son and realizes that they are unfamiliar with each other. Beneath the splendor of his success lies a man too war-torn to understand it. In fact, Billy's name, a diminutive form of William, indicates that he is more an immature boy than a man.

Vonnegut, then, injects the science-fiction thread, including the Tralfamadorians, to indicate how greatly the war has disrupted Billy's existence. It seems that Billy may be hallucinating about his experiences with the Tralfamadorians as a way to escape a world destroyed by war—a world that he cannot understand. Furthermore, the Tralfamadorian theory of the fourth dimension seems too convenient a device to be more than just a way for Billy to rational-ize all the death with he has seen face-to-face. Billy, then, is a trau-matized man who cannot come to terms with the destructiveness of war without invoking a far-fetched and impossible theory to which he can shape the world.

THE ILLUSION OF FREE WILL

In *Slaughterhouse-Five,* Vonnegut utilizes the Tralfamadorians, with their absurdly humorous toilet-plunger shape, to discuss the philosophical question of whether free will exists. These aliens live with the knowledge of the fourth dimension, which, they say, con-tains all moments of time occurring and reoccurring endlessly and simultaneously. Because they believe that all moments of time have already happened (since all moments repeat themselves endlessly), they possess an attitude of acceptance about their fates, figuring that they are powerless to change them. Only on Earth, according to the Tralfamadorians, is there talk of free will, since humans, they claim, mistakenly think of time as a linear progression.

Throughout his life, Billy runs up against forces that counter his free will. When Billy is a child, his father lets him sink into the deep end of a pool in order to teach him how to swim. Much to his father's dismay, however, Billy prefers the bottom of the pool, but, against his free will to stay there, he is rescued. Later, Billy is drafted into the war against his will. Even as a soldier, Billy is a joke, lacking training, supplies, and proper clothing. He bobs along like a puppet in Luxembourg, his civilian shoes flapping on his feet, and marches through the streets of Dresden draped in the remains of the scenery from a production of *Cinderella*.

Even while Vonnegut admits the inevitability of death, with or without war, he also tells us that he has instructed his sons not to participate in massacres or in the manufacture of machinery used to carry them out. But acting as if free will exists does not mean that it actually does. As Billy learns to accept the Tralfamadorian teach-ings, we see how his actions indicate the futility of free will. Even if Billy were to train hard, wear the proper uniform, and be a good sol-dier, he might still die like the others in Dresden who are much better soldiers than he. That he survives the incident as an improperly trained joke of a soldier is a testament to the deterministic forces that render free will and human effort an illusion.

The Importance of Sight

True sight is an important concept that is difficult to define for *Slaughterhouse-Five*. As an optometrist in Ilium, Billy has the professional duty of correcting the vision of his patients. If we extend the idea of seeing beyond the literal scope of Billy's profession, we can see that Vonnegut sets Billy up with several different lenses with which to correct the world's nearsightedness. One of the ways Billy can contribute to this true sight is through his knowledge of the fourth dimension, which he gains from the aliens at Tralfamadore. He believes in the Tralfamadorians' view of time—that all moments of time exist simultaneously and repeat themselves endlessly. He thus believes that he knows what will happen in the future (because everything has already happened and will continue to happen in the same way).

One can also argue, however, that Billy lacks sight completely. He goes to war, witnesses horrific events, and becomes mentally unstable as a result. He has a shaky grip on reality and at random moments experiences overpowering flashbacks to other parts of his life. His sense that aliens have captured him and kept him in a zoo before sending him back to Earth may be the product of an overactive imagination. Given all that Billy has been through, it is logical to believe that he has gone insane, and it makes sense to interpret these bizarre alien encounters as hallucinatory incidents triggered by mundane events that somehow create an association with past traumas. Looking at Billy this way, we can see him as someone who has lost true sight and lives in a cloud of hallucinations and self-doubt. Such a view creates the irony that one employed to correct the myopic view of others is actually himself quite blind.

Motifs

Motifs are recurring structures, contrasts, or literary devices that can help to develop and inform the text's major themes.

"So It Goes"

The phrase "So it goes" follows every mention of death in the novel, equalizing all of them, whether they are natural, accidental, or intentional, and whether they occur on a massive scale or on a very personal one. The phrase reflects a kind of comfort in the Tralfamadorian idea that although a person may be dead in a particular moment, he or she is alive in all the other moments of his or her life,

MOTIFS

which coexist and can be visited over and over through time travel. At the same time, though, the repetition of the phrase keeps a tally of the cumulative force of death throughout the novel, thus pointing out the tragic inevitability of death.

THE PRESENCE OF THE NARRATOR AS A CHARACTER

Vonnegut frames his novel with chapters in which he speaks in his own voice about his experience of war. This decision indicates that the fiction has an intimate connection with Vonnegut's life and convictions. Once that connection is established, however, Vonnegut backs off and lets the story of Billy Pilgrim take over. Throughout the book, Vonnegut briefly inserts himself as a character in the action: in the latrine at the POW camp, in the corpse mines of Dresden, on the phone when he mistakenly dials Billy's number. These appearances anchor Billy's life to a larger reality and highlight his struggle to fit into the human world.

SYMBOLS

Symbols are objects, characters, figures, or colors used to represent abstract ideas or concepts.

THE BIRD WHO SAYS "POO-TEE-WEET?"

The jabbering bird symbolizes the lack of anything intelligent to say about war. Birdsong rings out alone in the silence after a massacre, and *"Poo-tee-weet?"* seems about as appropriate a thing to say as any, since no words can really describe the horror of the Dresden firebombing. The bird sings outside of Billy's hospital window and again in the last line of the book, asking a question for which we have no answer, just as we have no answer for how such an atrocity as the firebombing could happen.

THE COLORS BLUE AND IVORY

On various occasions in *Slaughterhouse-Five,* Billy's bare feet are described as being blue and ivory, as when Billy writes a letter in his basement in the cold and when he waits for the flying saucer to kidnap him. These cold, corpselike hues suggest the fragility of the thin membrane between life and death, between worldly and otherworldly experience.

SUMMARY & ANALYSIS

CHAPTER 1

SUMMARY

> *It is so short and jumbled and jangled ... because there*
> *is nothing intelligent to say about a massacre.*
> (See QUOTATIONS, p. 45)

Vonnegut writes in his own voice, introducing his experience of the firebombing of Dresden, in eastern Germany, during World War II while he was a prisoner of war and his attempt for many years to complete a book on the subject. He begins with the claim that most of what follows is true, particularly the parts about war.

With funding from the Guggenheim Foundation, Vonnegut and his wartime friend Bernhard V. O'Hare return to Dresden in 1967. In a taxi on the way to the Dresden slaughterhouse that served as their prison, Vonnegut and O'Hare strike up a conversation with the cab driver about life under communism. It is to this man, Gerhard Müller, as well as to O'Hare's wife, Mary, that Vonnegut dedicates *Slaughterhouse-Five*. Müller later sends O'Hare a Christmas card with wishes for world peace.

Vonnegut relates his unsuccessful attempts to write about Dresden in the twenty-three years since he was there during the war. He is very proud of the outline of the story that he draws in crayon on the back of a roll of wallpaper. The wallpaper outline represents each character in a different color of crayon, with a line for each progressing through the story's chronology. Eventually the lines enter a zone of orange cross-hatching, which represents the firebombing, and those who survive the attack emerge and finally stop at the point when the POWs are returned. However, the outline does not help Vonnegut's writing. He initially expected to craft a masterpiece about this grave and immense subject, but, while the horrific destruction he witnessed occupies his mind over the years, it defies his attempts to capture it in writing. Vonnegut's antiwar stance only adds to the difficulty, since, as a filmmaker acquaintance remarks to him, writing a book against war would prevent war as effectively as writing a book against glaciers would prevent their motion.

Vonnegut recounts the events of his postwar life, including a stints as a student of anthropology at the University of Chicago, a police reporter, and a public relations man for General Electric in Schenectady, New York. In the years following the war, Vonnegut encounters ignorance about the magnitude of Dresden's destruction, and when he contacts the U.S. Air Force for information, he discovers that the event is still classified as top secret.

Around 1964, Vonnegut takes his young daughter and her friend with him to visit Bernhard V. O'Hare in Pennsylvania. He meets Mary O'Hare, who is disgusted by the likelihood that Vonnegut will portray himself and his fellow soldiers as manly heroes rather than the "babies" they were. With his right hand raised, Vonnegut vows not to glorify war and promises to call his book *The Children's Crusade*. Later that night he reads about the Children's Crusade and the earlier bombing of Dresden in 1760.

While teaching at the Iowa Writer's Workshop, Vonnegut lands a contract to write three books, of which *Slaughterhouse-Five* is to be the first. It is so short and jumbled, he explains, because there is nothing intelligent to say about a massacre.

On the way to Dresden, Vonnegut spends a night in a Boston hotel, where his perception of passing time becomes distorted, as if someone were playing with the clocks. He reads about the destruction of Sodom and Gomorrah in the bedside Gideon Bible and likens himself to Lot's wife, who against God's will looked back at the burning cities and was turned into a pillar of salt. Vonnegut muses on the book he has just written as an inevitable failure, and he resolves not to look back anymore.

ANALYSIS

The content of Chapter 1 in *Slaughterhouse-Five* makes it seem more like a preface to the novel than part of the novel itself. It is clearly autobiographical, and it exists on a plane different from that on which the bulk of the rest of the novel exists. In this chapter, Vonnegut forthrightly discusses his plan for the novel that we are about to read, and his statement of how the novel begins and how it ends would seem to indicate that he wrote Chapter 1 after writing the rest of the novel. His decision to make this contextual content part of the story rather than an introduction reflects how deeply entrenched his life is in the story that the novel relates, and perhaps how deeply entrenched the story that the novel relates is in his life.

By describing the process of writing *Slaughterhouse-Five* and the events surrounding its conception, Vonnegut makes himself a character in his own narrative. As he embeds an actual, external authorial presence within his text, he begins weaving the first of many threads into the story of Billy Pilgrim. In this chapter, Vonnegut says the words "So it goes" after relating that the mother of Gerhard Müller, the taxi driver, was incinerated in the Dresden attack. The phrase "So it goes" recurs throughout the novel, repeated after each report of a death. It becomes a mantra of resignation and acceptance. Because the phrase is first uttered by Vonnegut himself, each "So it goes" seems to come directly from the author and from the world outside the fiction of the text. When the narrator uses this phrase later on within the story, we can associate fact with fiction and also history with fantasy, as the sense of resignation and complacency experienced by Billy and other characters finds support in what seems like actual authority.

Vonnegut's narrative conception is intricate, as evidenced by his description of the wallpaper roll on which he outlines it, and the story docs not come to light until Vonnegut decides he can sacrifice the pleasant, organized outline for the true confusion entrenched in his war story. While Vonnegut finds his initial outline aesthetically pleasing—it constitutes a neat visual map of the structure that he will use to support his message of war's tragic, pointless irony—it is exactly this sort of structuring that has prevented Vonnegut from faithfully representing his subject matter through all his years of fruitless hard work. To convey the horror of his experience, he adopts a writing method that mirrors the circularity, confusion, and fatalism of his own feelings about the war. This fragmented structure persists throughout the novel, as protagonist Billy Pilgrim drifts back and forth in time.

Several passages in Chapter 1 suggest that aberrations of time play a pivotal role in Vonnegut's story. A lumberjack song whose last line also serves as its first, creating an endless loop, is an example of the circularity of time. Additionally, as Vonnegut waits in a Boston hotel room to leave for Dresden, time refuses to pass—it seems to him as though years drag by between twitches of his watch's second hand. Finally, the curious revelation, at the end of Chapter 1, of the novel's closing words invokes the idea of time as cyclical rather than linear—an idea that proves crucial to the novel's protagonist, Billy Pilgrim.

SUMMARY & ANALYSIS

CHAPTER 2

SUMMARY
The narrator bids us listen and declares that "Billy Pilgrim has come unstuck in time." Billy travels randomly through the moments of his life without control over his chronological destination. Born in 1922 in Ilium, New York, Billy grows up a funny-looking weakling. He graduates high school and trains to be an optometrist before being drafted. After his military service in Germany, he suffers from a nervous collapse and is treated with shock therapy. He recovers, marries, has two children, and becomes a wealthy optometrist.

In 1968, Billy survives a plane crash in Vermont; as he is recuperating, his wife dies in an accident. After returning home, Billy goes on a radio show in New York City to talk about his abduction by aliens in 1967. His twenty-one-year-old daughter, Barbara, discovers his proselytizing and brings him home, concerned for his sanity. The following month, Billy writes a letter to his local paper about the aliens.

The day the letter is published, Billy is hard at work on his second letter to the Ilium newspaper about lessons he learned when he was taken to the planet Tralfamadore. He is glowing with the expectation that his letter will console many people by explaining the true nature of time. Barbara is distraught by his behavior. She arrives at his house with newspaper in hand, unable to get Billy to talk sense.

Billy describes his entry into the army, his training as a chaplain's assistant in South Carolina, and his dazed trek behind enemy lines after the disastrous Battle of the Bulge in World War II. After the battle, Billy falls in with three other American soldiers, two of whom are scouts and capable soldiers. The one who is not, the anti-tank gunner Roland Weary, is a cruel, insecure man who saves Billy's life repeatedly in acts that he thinks will make him a hero.

Billy first time-shifts as he leans against a tree in a Luxembourg forest. He has fallen behind the others and has little will to continue. He swings through the extremes of his life: the violet light of death, the red light of pre-birth. He is then a small boy being thrown into the deep end of the YMCA swimming pool by his father, a proponent of the "sink-or-swim" method.

Billy time-travels to 1965. He is now forty-one years old and visiting his mother in a nursing home. He blinks and finds himself at a Little League banquet for his son, Robert, in 1958. He blinks again and opens his eyes at a party in 1961, cheating on his wife. Messily drunk, he passes out and wakes up again behind enemy lines. Roland Weary is shaking him awake.

The two scouts decide to ditch Weary and Billy, much to Weary's chagrin. All his life people have ditched him. He has imagined himself and the scouts as the Three Musketeers, and he blames Billy for breaking them up. Billy is suddenly giving a speech in 1957 as the newly elected president of the Ilium Lions Club. He is then back in the war, being captured by Germans along with Weary.

ANALYSIS

The narrative device of spastic time leads to a logical and emotional instability in the novel, likening our experience as readers to the experience Billy has in attempting to make sense of his life. We can thus understand how Billy feels as he skips uncontrollably through his life. By telling the beginning, middle, and end of the story right away, Vonnegut departs from the familiar literary signposts of cause and effect, suspense and climax. We do not see Billy as everyone else in his life sees him; rather, instead of seeing his life in a linear progression, understanding it moment by moment, we see the entirety of his life come together to define him. In other words, we can better understand and sympathize with Billy's dazed wandering through the totality of events that make up his existence.

Slaughterhouse-Five questions the possibility of human dignity in a century marked by unprecedented massacres and technological advancements in the machinery of mass murder. The initial stages of Billy's war experience reveal a man denied dignity. He lacks the proper accoutrements of a soldier, including military attire and loyal companions who would give their lives for him. Instead, Billy wears an absurd outfit and falls in with Roland Weary, who grudgingly saves Billy only to feed the delusional fantasy of his own heroism.

Weary, like the medieval crusaders and the Three Musketeers whom he idolizes, believes he is acting in dignified and exalted accordance with God's will. We see, however, that he actually has no more dignity than Billy. Vonnegut indicates here that war is war and death is death. Wars that seem like they are waged for religious or pious reasons seem to trickle down to pride, which is what motivates Weary despite the rhetoric about crusades and piety. The novel thus indicates one of war's most tragic ironies: that there can be no heroes without villains and victims, which makes even the most glorified aspects of war useless in the face of death.

Even as the chapter begins, with a matter-of-fact rundown of Billy's life story, Vonnegut confronts us with a litany of ironic deaths, each accompanied by the rhetorical shrug "So it goes." Billy's father dies in a hunting accident right before Billy ships overseas for combat; Billy is the only survivor in a plane full of optometrists when they crash into a mountain in Vermont; Billy's wife dies of accidental carbon monoxide poisoning on her way to visit him in the hospital after the plane crash. These deaths lend weight to the declaration in Chapter 1 by filmmaker Harrison Starr that an anti-war book is as ineffective as an anti-glacier book. An overarching irony in *Slaughterhouse-Five* is that death does not discriminate. We already know that Billy will survive war and a plane crash, despite the fact that he is ill suited to a life of danger and hardship.

CHAPTER 3

SUMMARY

> *Among the things Billy Pilgrim could not change were the past, the present, and the future.*
> *(See QUOTATIONS, p. 46)*

Weary and Billy's captors, a small group of German irregulars, take their valuables and discover an obscene photograph in Weary's pocket. As Billy lies in the snow, he sees an image of Adam and Eve in the polished boots of the commander. Weary must surrender his boots to a young German soldier, whose wooden clogs he receives in exchange. The two Americans are brought to a house full of other captives. Billy falls asleep and wakes up in 1967, in the middle of administering an eye examination. We learn that he has been falling asleep at work lately. He finishes with the patient and tries unsuccessfully to interest himself in an optometry article.

Billy closes his eyes and is once more a prisoner. He is roused and ordered to move. He joins a steady stream of POWs marching in the road outside. A German war photographer stages a capture scene of Billy emerging from a bush, surrendering to armed Germans. Billy slips back into 1967. He is driving on his way to a Lions Club luncheon through Ilium's black ghetto, still smoldering from recent riots, and then through a section gutted for urban renewal. The destruction he sees outside the car reminds him of the scene after the firebombing of Dresden. He drives a Cadillac with John Birch Society bumper stickers. His son, Robert, is a Green Beret in Vietnam. His daughter, Barbara, is about to get married. He is quite wealthy.

At the Lions Club meeting, a marine major speaks about bombing in North Vietnam. Billy has no opinion on this subject. He has a plaque on his office wall that helps guide him through such listlessness. It reads: "God grant me the serenity to accept the things I cannot change, courage to change the things I can, and wisdom always to tell the difference."

After the luncheon, Billy returns to his stately home. He lies down for a nap and finds himself weeping. A bed vibrator called "Magic Fingers," purchased to help Billy fall asleep, jiggles him while he weeps. He closes his eyes and is back in Luxembourg, marching. The wind makes his eyes water. Weary marches ahead of him, his feet raw and bloody from his ill-fitting clogs. The prisoners march into Germany and are taken to a railroad yard. A mentally unstable colonel who has lost his whole regiment asks if Billy is one of his men. The colonel, who likes to be called "Wild Bob," tells Billy, "If you're ever in Cody, Wyoming, just ask for Wild Bob!" The soldiers are sorted by rank and placed in crowded boxcars. They must take turns sleeping and standing, and they pass a helmet as a chamber pot. Billy is separated from Weary. His train does not move for two days. When the train begins to roll toward the interior, Billy travels to the night he is kidnapped by the Tralfamadorians.

―――――――――――――

ANALYSIS

Although the Serenity Prayer, inscribed on the plaque in Billy's optometry office, is an optimistic statement, it is undermined by the text's comment that "[a]mong the things Billy Pilgrim could not change were the past, the present, and the future." Such a comment plays up *Slaughterhouse-Five*'s suggestion that any attempt to change life is futile—that prayers and the invocation of supposed higher beings cannot alter Billy's immutable past, present, and future. Though Billy enjoys the illusion of free will, since his existence is characterized by all the components seemingly necessary for happiness—a family, a comfortable home, and a successful business—life is still meaningless for him. What he does not understand until his abduction by aliens in 1967 is that he has no more chosen a wife or a career in optometry than he has chosen to be born a weakling. Vonnegut wryly lists the past, the present, and the future as if they were small and inconsequential items on a long laundry list detailing everything that neither Billy nor God can change.

At this point in the novel, Billy shows signs of the strain that comes from the hopelessness of war. He lacks the ability to control his time-tripping, and he is often overcome by quiet bouts of spontaneous and unexplainable weeping. Additionally, he suffers from severe sleep disorders: he falls asleep in the middle of examining patients, but once he is in bed he needs the help of a Magic Fingers vibrator to fall asleep. Historically speaking, the trauma of war frequently causes mental disorders in soldiers who return from the front. This was true of soldiers who participated in World War II as well as in other conflicts. Their symptoms, evidence of mental illness, are typically characterized as post-traumatic stress disorder. The mental problems that Billy manifests thus lend an undercurrent of unreliability to his perspective.

But the prospect that Billy is mentally ill should not compel us to dismiss the events and stories in the novel as the ramblings of a madman. Insanity extends beyond Billy himself, infiltrating the world in which he lives. For instance, Vonnegut appears intermittently as a character, not only in Billy's war experiences but also on the night of Billy's abduction by aliens. Billy's hallucination of the image of Adam and Eve in the boots of his commander does not spring wholly from his brain; earlier, the commander himself invokes Adam and Eve as he holds up his boots to demonstrate their high polish. It becomes clear, then, that characters' psychologies and mental states overlap in a realm of dementia. It is impossible to ridicule Billy's thoughts or words as insane ramblings, since his world contains such illogical and unexplainable events. Furthermore, the anonymous narrator, who at times sounds like Vonnegut himself, may be a participant in this frenzy of insanity, blurring the boundaries between reality and fantasy.

CHAPTER 4

SUMMARY

There was a drunk on the other end. Billy could almost smell his breath—mustard gas and roses.

(See QUOTATIONS, *p. 47)*

On the night of his daughter's wedding day, Billy cannot sleep. Because he has traveled in time already, he knows he will be kidnapped by the Tralfamadorians' flying saucer in an hour. Billy gets out of bed by the light of a full moon and wanders down the hallway and into his daughter's empty bedroom. The phone rings, and Billy hears the voice of a drunk who has dialed the wrong number. He can almost catch the scent of mustard gas and roses on the man's breath.

Downstairs, Billy picks up a half-empty bottle of champagne from a table. He watches a late-night documentary on American bombers and their gallant pilots in World War II. Slightly unstuck in time, Billy watches the movie forward and backward. Planes fly backward, magically quelling flames, drawing their fragmented bombs into steel containers, and sucking them back up into their bellies. Guns on the ground suck metal fragments from the pilots, crew, and planes. Weapons are shipped backed to factories, where they are carefully disassembled and broken down into their constituent minerals. The minerals are shipped to specialists all over the world who "hide them cleverly" in the ground, "so they never hurt anybody ever." In Billy's mind, Hitler becomes a baby and all of humanity works toward creating two perfect people named Adam and Eve.

Billy heads out to the backyard to meet the saucer that will arrive soon. A sound like a melodious owl heralds the arrival of the spacecraft, which is 100 feet in diameter. Once on board, Billy is asked if he has any questions. He asks, "Why me?"—a question that his captors think very typical of earthlings to ask. They tell him that there is no why, since the moment simply is and since all of them are trapped in the moment, like bugs in amber.

Billy is then anesthetized. The crush of the spaceship's acceleration sends him hurtling through time. He is back on a boxcar traveling across Germany. The men take turns sleeping and standing. No one wants to let Billy sleep beside him because Billy yells and kicks in his sleep. He thus sleeps standing up.

By the ninth day of the boxcar journey, people are dying. Roland Weary, who is in another car, dies after making sure that everyone in the car knows who is responsible for his death: Billy Pilgrim. A car thief from Cicero, Illinois, named Paul Lazzaro swears he will make Billy pay for causing Weary's death.

On the tenth night, the train reaches its destination: a prison camp. The prisoners are issued coats, their clothes are deloused, and they are led to a mass shower. Among the prisoners is Edgar Derby, a forty-four-year-old teacher from Indianapolis. When the water begins to flow in the shower, Billy time-travels to his infancy. His mother has just given him a bath. He is then a middle-aged optometrist playing golf with three other optometrists. He sinks a putt, bends down to pick it up, and is back on the flying saucer. He asks where he is and how he got there. A voice reiterates that he is trapped in a blob of amber. He is where he is because the moment is structured that way, because time in general is structured that way—because it could not be otherwise. The voice, which is Tralfamadorian, comments that only on Earth is there talk of free will.

Only on Earth is there any talk of free will.

(See QUOTATIONS, *p.* 48*)*

ANALYSIS

The Tralfamadorian concept of time emphasizes the role of fate in shaping existence and completely rejects free will. When Billy is kidnapped, he understands that all people and things are trapped in life's collection of moments like bugs trapped in amber. Billy is locked into his fate; any resistance to this notion is futile. Billy's question "Why me?" reveals the limits of human consciousness; the Tralfamadorians would never think to ask such a question, since they know that the structure of time is beyond anyone's control. What is important, then, is how one interprets the events in one's life, which certainly changes for Billy after he returns from the war.

The fact that Billy's death is determined years before it happens is further support for the Tralfamadorian argument that we are locked into our fate. Roland Weary dies blaming Billy and making sure everyone in his boxcar knows the name of Billy Pilgrim. Though Billy is starved, sick, and half-dead, we know that he will not die in the boxcar, the prison camp, or even in the city of Dresden. He will die because one deluded and solitary human being, Paul Lazzaro, keeps a promise over the course of thirty years to avenge the death of Roland Weary. In the novel's moral hierarchy, revenge ranks almost as high as war as a justification for propagating absurd and pointless death. Billy's death, as we come to see it, is a result of nothing but sheer stupidity and pride on the part of a single human being. This description, on a larger scale, can easily be adapted to describe war: the mass mortality of war results from large-scale ignorance and stupidity coupled with an unrelenting, shameless sense of pride.

One of the novel's many quiet, understated mockeries of war occurs early in this chapter, when Billy sits down to watch a war movie, and, as a result of his time perception, watches it backward. The events portrayed in the movie, when viewed in a different order, take on a different meaning. By rewinding the war, Billy transforms warmongering motives into peace-loving ones. This reversal demonstrates that chronological order is significant; it resurrects the idea of cause-and-effect relationships in a challenge to the Tralfamadorian denial that time is linear. Billy's backward viewing of the movie contradicts the idea that moments are structured a certain way no matter the order in which you perceive them. This notion lends weight to Vonnegut's decision to manipulate the conception of time in *Slaughterhouse-Five,* which can be seen as a story in which the meaning changes according to the order of events.

CHAPTER 5

SUMMARY

> *There isn't any particular relationship between the messages.... There is no beginning, no middle, no end, no suspense, no moral....*
> (See QUOTATIONS, *p. 49*)

In his zoo enclosure, Billy reads the novel *Valley of the Dolls,* the only earthling book available. He learns that Tralfamadorian books are composed of short telegram-like clumps of symbols separated by stars. Billy skips back to two childhood scenes during a family tour of the American West, then to the prison camp in Germany. After the prisoners are showered and their clothes are deloused, their names are entered in a ledger, and they are officially alive again.

The Americans are housed with a group of British officers who have accidentally received extra provisions. The Brits welcome the Americans with a cheerful banquet but quickly become disgusted with the sorry state of the enlisted men. During a performance of *Cinderella,* Billy laughs uncontrollably and is taken to the camp's "hospital." He is drugged and wakes up in 1948, in the mental ward of a veterans' hospital in New York.

Billy has committed himself to the mental ward in his last year of optometry school. In the aftermath of war, he finds life meaningless. In the bed next to him lies an ex-captain named Eliot Rosewater. Eliot introduces Billy to the clever but poorly written science-fiction novels of a writer named Kilgore Trout. Billy's mother visits him, and he covers his head with a blanket.

Back in Germany, Edgar Derby keeps watch over Billy's sickbed. Billy remembers Derby's death by firing squad, which happens in the near future. Billy travels back to the veterans' hospital. His fiancée, Valencia Merble, is visiting. They discuss Kilgore Trout with Rosewater.

Billy time-travels to his geodesic dome in the zoo on Tralfamadore, outfitted with Sears Roebuck furniture and appliances. The Tralfamadorians tell Billy that there are actually seven sexes among humans, all of which are necessary for reproduction. Since five of these sexes are active only in the fourth dimension, Billy cannot perceive them. When Billy praises the peacefulness of Tralfamadore, the aliens inform him that Tralfamadorians are at war sometimes and at peace at others. They add that they know how the universe will end: one of their pilots will accidentally blow it up. It always happens the same way and that is how the moment is structured. They state that war cannot be prevented on Tralfamadore any more than it can on Earth.

Billy skips back to his wedding night with Valencia in Cape Ann, Massachusetts. After they make love, Valencia asks Billy about the war. He gets up and goes to the bathroom and finds himself back in his hospital bed in the prison camp. Billy wanders to the latrine, where the American soldiers are violently sick. One of them is Kurt Vonnegut.

The next morning, Paul Lazzaro appears at the hospital, knocked unconscious after trying to steal from an Englishman. A German major reads aloud a monograph on the pathetic state of American soldiers by Howard W. Campbell, Jr., an American playwright turned Nazi propagandist.

Billy falls asleep and wakes up in 1968, back at work on his letter to the paper. His daughter, Barbara, scolds him, notices that it is cold in the house, and leaves to call the oil-burner man after putting Billy to bed. Lying under his electric blanket, Billy travels to Tralfamadore, just as an actress named Montana Wildhack arrives and goes into hysterics. She has been brought to Tralfamadore to be Billy's mate. Eventually she grows to trust him, and soon they are sleeping together.

Billy wakes up in 1968, having just had a wet dream about Montana Wildhack. The next day, Billy examines a boy whose father has been killed in Vietnam. He shares Tralfamadorian insights with the boy, whose mother realizes that Billy is insane. Billy's daughter is called to take him home.

ANALYSIS

As he begins his stay with the Tralfamadorians, Billy learns about their concept of time and their philosophy of acceptance. If there is no free will, and if each moment is structured so that it can only occur the way it occurs, then it makes sense to accept things as they come. Reconciliation to the world, or the "So it goes" attitude, comes from visiting all the moments of one's life innumerable times. The moment of death is no more permanent than any other moment. This realization comes as a great comfort to Billy, given the horrible killing he has witnessed. Since it offers him immediate comfort, he makes a willed decision to share his insights with the world when the time is ripe. By offering the Tralfamadorian theories to the public, Billy figuratively extends his optometry practice beyond typical lenses and spectacles, correcting humankind's understanding of death and will. Billy's desire to share his story with the public, however, is a matter of personal will. Ironically, Billy concertedly exercises his free will in order to teach others that free will is futile.

Despite this irony, Billy is yet unaware that there is danger in a world without free will, especially when no one claims responsibility for his or her actions. When a German guard knocks down an American prisoner and the baffled man asks, "Why me?" the German shoots back, "Vy you? Vy anybody?" This reply echoes the Tralfamadorian answer to the same question from Billy when he is abducted. In the veterans' hospital, Rosewater and Billy brood fatalistically about the state of their universe, and Kilgore Trout's science fiction provides a welcome escape.

The lighthearted Tralfamadorian touches in *Slaughterhouse-Five,* such as the aliens' resemblance to toilet plungers or the ridiculous showroom in which they house Billy, temper the devastation of the war scenes. But by putting the aliens' philosophy in the mouth of the brutal German soldier, Vonnegut also uses science fiction to caution us about the consequences of escapism.

Billy accepts the Tralfamadorian advice to look at life's nice moments as much as possible. He still does not control his time travel, but he takes comfort in the foreknowledge he gains from it. For example, when Valencia declares that she will lose weight for Billy, he assures her that he likes her the way she is. Billy actually thinks Valencia is ugly, but he knows from his time travels that his marriage to her will be comfortable.

Billy's revelations about Tralfamadore lead us to question his sanity. It seems possible that Tralfamadore is something that he merely imagines, especially since he begins reading Kilgore Trout's science fiction at a stage in which he feels he is losing whatever grip he has on reality. He is already unable to live fully in the present and unable to control his movements backward and forward through time. Science fiction helps him and Rosewater as they attempt to "reinvent themselves and reinvent their universe." Perhaps Billy, unable to change the fact that he cannot live his life normally after the war, salvages his sanity by inventing a new understanding of the nature of time. The Tralfamadorians, who are strongly reminiscent of some of Trout's creations, conveniently explain how the whole thing works and serve as a model for coping in a four-dimensional universe. People who invent new understandings of the nature of time are seldom considered sane, but in his own mind, Billy is at peace. Billy probably suffers from both disillusionment from the war and delusions. While the delusions may outweigh his disillusionment in terms of his mental well-being, they perhaps allow him to function, at least part of the time, in the normal working world.

CHAPTER 6

SUMMARY

After spending the night on morphine, Billy wakes at dawn in his prison bed on the day he and the other Americans are to be transported to Dresden. He senses something radiating energy near his bed and discovers the source of this "animal magnetism": two small lumps inside the lining of his overcoat. A telepathic communication informs him that the lumps can work miracles for him if he does not try to find out any more about them.

Billy dozes off and wakes again later the same morning. With him are Edgar Derby and Paul Lazzaro. The English officers are building themselves a new latrine, having abandoned the old one to the sick Americans. The Englishman who beat up Lazzaro stops by, and Lazzaro tells him that he is going to have the officer killed after the war. The sweetest thing in life, he claims, is revenge. He says that one time he fed a dog that had bitten him a steak filled with sharp pieces of metal and watched it die in torment. Lazzaro reminds Billy of Roland Weary's final wish and advises him not to answer the doorbell after the war.

Billy says he already knows that he will die because an old, crazed Lazzaro will keep his promise. He has time-traveled to this moment many times, and he knows that he will be a messianic figure by that time, delivering a speech about the nature of time to a stadium crowd of admirers and granting them solace by sharing the understanding that moments last forever and that death is a negligible reality. He speaks at a baseball park covered by a geodesic dome. It is 1976, and China has dropped a hydrogen bomb on Chicago. The United States has been divided into twenty nations to prevent it from threatening the world. Moments after he predicts his own death and closes his speech with the words "Farewell, hello, farewell, hello," Billy is killed by an assassin's high-powered laser gun. He experiences the violet nothingness of death, and then he swings back into life and to early 1945. The record of these events, Billy says, he has recorded on a cassette that he has left in a safe-deposit box in a bank.

After a lecture on personal hygiene by an Englishman and an election in which Edgar Derby is named their leader, the Americans are shipped to Dresden. Arrayed in his fur-satin coat and swathed in cloth scraps and silver boots left over from the production of *Cinderella*, Billy looks like the war's unwitting clown. When the boxcars open, the Americans gaze on the most beautiful city they have ever seen. "Oz," says Kurt Vonnegut, who is in the boxcar too. Eight sorry, broken-down German soldiers guard one hundred American prisoners. They are marched through the city to a former slaughterhouse that will serve as their quarters. Billy is amazed by Dresden's architecture. The city is relatively untouched by war, with industries and recreational facilities still operating. All the citizens are amused by the ragtag parade, except one, who finds Billy's ridiculous appearance offensive. The man is insulted by Billy's lack of dignity and his apparent reduction of the war to a joke or pageant.

SUMMARY & ANALYSIS

ANALYSIS

Billy's discovery of two mysterious lumps inside the lining of his overcoat can be better understood in relation to the biblical story of Lot's wife mentioned in Chapter 1, when Vonnegut opens the Gideon Bible and reads the story of the destruction of Sodom and Gomorrah. Although the firebombing of Dresden can be seen as a modern tale of fire and brimstone—ultimate destruction on the ground wrought by a faraway unseen force—the part of the tale of Sodom and Gomorrah that interests Vonnegut most is the story of Lot's wife, who looks back at the destruction even though she is told not to and is turned into a pillar of salt as punishment. Vonnegut praises her for knowing her fate and looking back anyway. The tale provides a counterpoint to Billy, who is content and grateful for the existence of the lumps and feels an almost inhuman lack of curiosity and temptation to find out more, to see them with his own eyes. The lumps seem to radiate a living force, but as long as Billy leaves them undisturbed, he lets part of his humanity lie dormant. The story creates a polarity between Billy and Lot's wife, with Billy being the disillusioned man who escapes to his delusions and Lot's wife the determined woman who stares her own destruction in the face. For Vonnegut, the war functions in the same way that the wantonness of Sodom and Gomorrah does—it is a force that condemns those it touches to one of two fates. On one side, Lot's wife knows that looking back at the city will immobilize her, yet she is determined to take her last glance; on the other side, Billy accepts that he must avoid being curious about the war, since its effects would immobilize him, and instead must go through life with the delusion that there is no need to worry, since whatever will be already *is*.

However, the narrative technique in these chapters suggests that Billy's future is not absolutely determined. The narrator's tone shifts slightly when relating Billy's account of 1976. Distancing himself from Billy's own statements, the narrator is not exactly skeptical, but he adopts a disclaimer-like attitude. Instead of reporting the world events and the details of Billy's assassination in his own voice, the narrator relays the transcript of Billy's tape, opening the account with "Billy Pilgrim says. . . ." in order to make clear that it is Billy, not the narrator, saying what follows. *Slaughterhouse-Five* is, after all, an earthling's approximation of a Tralfamadorian tale, and it is therefore subject to the limits of human perception and human skepticism. The narration, which earlier functions as a sense of external authority and support, now creates distance between us and the story, and this distance confuses our sense of what we can trust and believe.

CHAPTER 7

SUMMARY

Nearly twenty-five years after his experience in Dresden, Billy boards a chartered plane with twenty-eight other optometrists, including his father-in-law, headed for a trade conference in Montreal. Valencia waves goodbye from the tarmac while eating a candy bar. The narrator informs us that, according to the Tralfamadorians, Valencia and her father, like every other animal and plant, are both machines. Billy knows that the plane will crash. A barbershop quartet of optometrists called the Four-eyed Bastards serenades the passengers with bawdy tunes. One of them is a Polish song about coal miners, which makes Billy remember a public hanging he witnessed in Dresden in which a Polish man was lynched for having sex with a German woman.

Billy dozes off and drifts back to a moment in 1944. Roland Weary is shaking him; Billy tells the Three Musketeers to go on without him.

The plane crashes into Sugarbush Mountain in Vermont, and Billy survives with a fractured skull. Austrian ski instructors wearing black ski masks arrive on the scene. As they check for signs of life, Billy whispers "Schlachthof-fünf" ("Slaughterhouse-Five" in German), a phrase he learned in Dresden in order to communicate the address of his prison if he got lost. The ski instructors transport Billy down the mountain on a toboggan. A famous neurosurgeon operates on him, and Billy remains unconscious for two days. The narrator tells us that Billy's convalescence is filled with dreams, some of them involving time travel. He goes back to Dresden and his first evening at the slaughterhouse, when he, Edgar Derby, and their young German guard Werner Gluck accidentally open a door onto a shower room full of beautiful naked girls. This incident marks the first glimpse of female nudity that Billy and Gluck have ever had. The three men finally make it to their intended destination, the prison kitchen. The cook regards their sorry condition and declares, "All the real soldiers are dead."

Another Dresden time trip after his plane accident takes Billy to a factory that manufactures malt syrup. The POWs work there making the molasses-like concoction intended to serve as a nutritional supplement for pregnant women. All the malnourished prisoners who work at the factory secretly eat the syrup themselves, scooping it out of vats with spoons hidden in every corner of the building. Billy takes his first spoonful on his second day at work, and his scrawny body shivers with "ravenous gratitude." Billy hands a syrupy spoon through a window to Edgar Derby, who is working outside. Upon tasting the syrup, Derby bursts into tears of joy.

ANALYSIS

The philosophy of the Tralfamadorians is reminiscent of a principle of Einsteinian physics. Einstein argued that an object is described by four coordinates: the three spatial dimensions and time. Put simply, in order to know where something is, one must know *when* it is. Because objects change over time, true descriptions of an object require describing it at every moment. The kinds of descriptions we give are merely snapshots that convey an object as it appears at a given point in time. The true nature of the object is expressed only by the totality of snapshots taken throughout the object's history and its future.

In effect, *Slaughterhouse-Five* proposes that the same thing could be said of a person. The Tralfamadorians, who see in four dimensions, perceive all of an object and all of a person, whereas humans do not. But Billy's rapid, relentless time-tripping approximates this ability to perceive holistically. This dimensional quality of perception is particularly present in Chapter 7, when Billy goes on a series of rapid-fire time trips while recovering from his head injury. We never see Billy wholly at any one moment, as Vonnegut does not engage in typical character description. Instead, we catch brief glimpses of very different Billy Pilgrims from very different moments. We try to grasp the sum of all the different Billy Pilgrims from all the different moments through quick, alternating glimpses of his past, present, and future. But one dilemma that surfaces in attempting to discern which Billy is the *real* Billy is the possibility that perhaps he is just a summation of all his different snapshots. Billy's value as a character, then, might be in sync with the value of *Slaughterhouse-Five* as a whole: it is less important to try to understand Billy and the novel as coherent entities than to recognize the scope and significance of their respective journeys.

Vonnegut also creates a curious distinction between true time travel and dreams. He tells us that "Billy was unconscious for two days after that, and he dreamed millions of things, some of them true. The true things were time-travel." This last sentence suggests an interpretation of Billy's spastic tripping through time that saves him from a verdict of insanity. Instead, we can understand his time travel as dreams about his real life. Billy, like most people, has some dreams that are like memories of real-life events and some that are fantastical fabrications. Time travel may just be a label for the dreams about real-life events to suggest how powerful these dreams are. If we take this interpretation to its logical conclusion, most of

Slaughterhouse-Five would qualify as one big dream in Billy's head. Of course, we may still believe that Billy has a sleep disorder if he can drift off into dreams while standing up in the forest, standing behind his optometer at work, speaking to the Lions Club, or visiting the bathroom after making love to his wife on their wedding night. Over the course of the novel, we actually encounter very few dreams that would not qualify as time travel. These include the time that Billy dreams he is a giraffe and the occasion on which he daydreams about doing tricks for a crowd by sliding around on a smooth floor in gym socks.

CHAPTER 8

SUMMARY

Howard W. Campbell, Jr., the American Nazi propagandist, speaks to the weary, malnourished prisoners at the slaughterhouse. He solicits them to join his Free American Corps to fight on the Russian front, promising food and repatriation after the war. Edgar Derby stands up and, in his finest moment, denounces Campbell. He defends the American fight for freedom and praises the brotherhood between Russians and Americans. An air-raid siren concludes the confrontation, and everyone takes shelter in a meat locker carved into the bedrock beneath the slaughterhouse. The alarm is false. The narrator states that Dresden will not be destroyed until the next night.

Billy dozes off in the meat locker and travels back to a conversation with his exasperated daughter, Barbara. She blames Kilgore Trout for Billy's Tralfamadorian pronouncements. Billy recalls the first time he mets Trout in his own hometown of Ilium. Trout manages newspaper delivery boys for the *Ilium Gazette*. He is shocked that Billy has read his books. Billy invites Trout to his eighteenth wedding anniversary celebration, where Trout is a hit with the optometrists and their wives. One of them, the credulous and attractive Maggie White, listens with concern as Trout leads her to believe that publishing made-up stories qualifies as a fraud punishable by God and worthy of jail time. In his enthusiasm, Trout accidentally spits a piece of salmon roe into Maggie's cleavage.

The Four-eyed Bastards (or Febs), the barbershop quartet made up of optometrists, sing a sentimental song about old friendship. The experience of watching and listening to them visibly shakes Billy. Trout guesses that Billy has looked through a "time window."

When the barbershop quartet sings again, Billy has to leave the room. He goes upstairs, where he accidentally walks in on his son in the bathroom holding a guitar as he sits on the toilet. Billy lies down on his bed, trying to figure out why the Febs have such an effect on him. He remembers the night Dresden was destroyed. The American prisoners and four guards waited out the bombing in the meat locker. They emerged to find Dresden replaced by one big, smoking mineral deposit. The four guards huddled together, and the changing expressions on their faces—silent mouths open in awe and terror—seem to Billy like a silent film of a barbershop quartet.

Billy time-travels to Tralfamadore, where Montana Wildhack, who is six months pregnant, asks him to tell her a story. He tells her of the destruction of Dresden and of the little burned logs lying all around that were actually people. In bombed-out Dresden, the guards and the prisoners venture out onto the moonscape to forage for food and water. In the city itself they do not encounter another living soul. At nightfall, they reach an inn in a portion of a suburb untouched by bombs or flames. The blind innkeeper and his family know that Dresden has been destroyed. They give the prisoners soup and beer and a stable to sleep in for the night. As the prisoners prepare for bed, the innkeeper says in German, "Good night, Americans. Sleep well."

ANALYSIS

Billy's realization that he is hiding his secret history of trauma from himself marks an important point in the novel. Despite the fact that Vonnegut has dispensed with most traditional narrative devices in *Slaughterhouse-Five*, the focusing of Billy's self-awareness constitutes a crucial moment in the development of Billy's character. It paves the way for his eventual decision to spread the Tralfamadorian gospel on earth. Ironically, instead of sitting back and accepting human ignorance of the true nature of time, Billy exerts his will to help his fellow inhabitants of earth.

Billy's recognition of the effect of the Febs on his psyche demonstrates a great deal of self-awareness. Although he undergoes emotional stress in this section, his response is not to travel in time, as it has been in other chapters. The fact that he stays rooted in the present suggests that this moment is one of Billy's sanest, even though he is suffering from tremendous emotional anguish. When Trout asks Billy if he has seen the past or the future through a "time window," Billy answers no. Valencia hits closer to the mark when she says, "You looked as though you'd seen a *ghost.*" The sight of the Febs with their mouths open in song raises the specter of a tragic memory. As Billy retires to his room to attempt to sort out the cause of his distress, he remembers (without time-tripping, as the narrator takes pains to point out) the horrible sight of the four German guards, clustered together with their mouths agape.

The Febs' singing provides Billy with a long-delayed catharsis for the tragedy that he seems to have passively observed in Dresden. In fact, Billy experienced the actual firebombing as no more than the sound of heavy footsteps above the safe haven of the meat locker. Seeing the Febs and remembering the sight of his German guards, Billy is finally able to create an association with the tragedy. Four open-mouthed men signify for Billy the loss of tens of thousands of lives. Realizing this fact allows him to grieve the loss and discuss it openly with Montana Wildhack when she asks for a story. By contrast, when Valencia questions Billy about the war on their wedding night, he tells her nothing because he cannot yet understand his own experience, much less recount it to others.

With his discovery that he has been keeping a secret from himself, a window opens for Billy not onto time but onto another facet of his personality. Similarly, Billy accidentally illuminates another side of his son, Robert, when he opens the bathroom door and discovers him sitting on the toilet with his pants around his ankles and a pink guitar slung around his neck. Billy comes to the important realization that although he likes his son, he barely knows him. It is as if Billy has partially awakened to the world around him and its potential for human relationships.

CHAPTER 9

SUMMARY

A hysterical Valencia drives to the hospital where Billy is recovering from the plane crash. She hits another car on the way and drives from the scene of the accident without a functioning exhaust system. She pulls up in front of the hospital and passes out from carbon monoxide poisoning. Her face is bright blue. She dies one hour later.

Billy is unconscious, time-traveling and oblivious to his wife's passing. In the next bed, an arrogant Harvard history professor named Bertram Copeland Rumfoord is recovering from a skiing accident. Rumfoord is the official Air Force historian, and he is working on a condensed history of the U.S. Army Air Corps in

World War II. He has to write a section on the smashing success of Dresden's bombing, despite the fact that some of his sources characterize it as an unnecessary carnage.

When Billy first regains consciousness, everyone thinks the accident has left him a vegetable. But behind his catatonic facade he is preparing to tell the world about Tralfamadore and to explain the true nature of time. Billy tells Rumfoord that he was in Dresden for the firebombing, but the professor doesn't want to listen. Billy then travels back to a May afternoon in Dresden, two days before the end of the war.

Many Germans have fled because they heard that the Russians were coming. Billy and a few other prisoners find a green, coffin-shaped wagon hitched to two horses, and they fill it with food and souvenirs. Outside the slaughterhouse, Billy remains in the wagon and dozes in the sun. It is a happy moment in his life. The sound of a middle-aged German couple talking about the horses awakens him. The animals' mouths are bleeding, their hooves are broken, and they are dying of thirst. Billy has been oblivious to their poor condition until now. The couple makes Billy get out and look at the animals, and he begins to cry his first tears of the war.

Back in the hospital the next day, Rumfoord quizzes Billy about Dresden. Billy's daughter, Barbara, arrives and takes him home. She places him under the care of a live-in nurse. Billy's message cannot wait any longer. He sneaks out and drives to New York City to tell the world about Tralfamadore.

Once in the city, Billy goes to Times Square. He sees four Kilgore Trout books in the window of an adult bookstore and goes in to read them. One of the books is about an earthling man and woman who are kidnapped by aliens and taken to a zoo on a faraway planet. While inside the shop, Billy glimpses the headline of a pornographic magazine: "What really became of Montana Wildhack?" He also sees a few seconds of a pornographic movie starring a teen-aged Montana.

There happens to be a radio station near Billy's hotel. Claiming to be a writer from the *Ilium Gazette,* Billy gets on a talk-show panel of literary critics discussing the state of the novel. Billy waits his turn, then speaks about Tralfamadore and Montana Wildhack and the nature of time. He is escorted to the street and makes his way back to his hotel. There he falls asleep and time-travels back to Tralfamadore, where Montana is breast-feeding their child. She says that she can tell that Billy has been time-traveling. A silver locket hanging between her bare breasts bears the same inscription—the Serenity Prayer—as the plaque in Billy's optometry office.

ANALYSIS

Vonnegut throws the tragic absurdity of human life into sharp relief in his description of Billy's happiest moment. The day after the German surrender, Billy dozes blissfully in the sun amid Dresden's ruins, but he is lying in a tomb on wheels. The coffin-shaped wagon points to a symbolic death suffered even by the survivors of war. It is the death of a meaningful existence, the death of innocence for all the "babies" who carry out the latest Children's Crusade. Billy has not yet grasped the emptiness of victory. Yet when two Germans point out the miserable state of the horses hitched to Billy's coffin, he cannot avoid the fact that his victory also contains his own defeat. The happiest moment in Billy's life ends in tears for the plight of two beleaguered beasts of burden.

Billy's interaction with the historian in the Vermont hospital shows how history and fiction are to some degree interchangeable in *Slaughterhouse-Five*. Although Billy's stories of time travel and alien abduction are clearly spurious, it is still possible that he has been a soldier in World War II. But when the official author of Dresden's history of destruction dismisses Billy's claim of having witnessed it, it becomes clear that our conception of history is shaped by the people who are in charge of writing about it. The world knows little about the massive and grisly loss of civilian life at Dresden, and it is partly up to Rumford to keep it that way. He would rather not hear what he fears Billy might have to say about the events. *Slaughterhouse-Five* is Vonnegut's offensive against the collective amnesia propagated by people like Rumford.

The things Billy sees when he visits the bookstore in Times Square further confuse our understanding of reality within the novel's fictional framework. Books by Kilgore Trout are displayed mysteriously in the store's window, making us wonder whether or not it is a coincidence that Billy looks at the Trout book about aliens abducting a man and a woman right before he tells a nighttime radio audience about an experience of his own similar to what Trout's book describes. When Billy brings the book to the front of the store, the clerks react with bewilderment—they do not even know that they carry Trout novels. The books take on a fantastical aura; it seems possible that they have been placed by an alien hand for Billy's eyes only, to open him up to a new consciousness. Or, perhaps, Vonnegut is removing the credibility with which Billy's story begins. We see similar stories of alien abduction in other Trout novels within *Slaughterhouse-Five,* and Billy also sees pornographic movies starring Montana Wildhack that portray her as a captive in an alien zoo. These late mentions of such material suggest that Billy's life with Montana in the Tralfamadorian zoo might not be a lucid memory or an instance of time travel but rather a delusion that incorporates elements that Billy has encountered in fictional works.

CHAPTER 10

SUMMARY

It is 1968. Robert Kennedy and Martin Luther King, Jr. are both dead, assassinated within a month of one another. Body counts from the jungle war in Vietnam fill the evening news.

According to Billy, Tralfamadorians are more interested in Darwin than in Jesus Christ. They admire the Darwinian view that death serves a function and that "corpses are improvements." A Kilgore Trout book, *The Big Board,* features aliens who capture an earthling and ask him about Darwin and golf.

Vonnegut tells us that he is not overjoyed if what Billy learned from the Tralfamadorians about eternal existence is true. Still, he is grateful for all the pleasant times experienced in his life. Vonnegut recalls one of those moments—his return to Dresden with his war buddy O'Hare. On the plane, the men eat salami sandwiches and drink white wine, and the author's friend shows him a book that claims the world population will reach seven billion by the year 2000. "I suppose they will all want dignity," Vonnegut remarks.

Billy is also back in Dresden, two days after the war, digging for bodies. Vonnegut and O'Hare are there too. After spending two nights in the stable, the prisoners are put to work excavating the ruins of Dresden, where they discover innumerable "corpse mines." The bodies rot faster than they can be removed, making for a grisly cleanup job. One prisoner, a Maori, dies of the dry heaves. Eventually, as the pace of putrefaction outstrips the recovery efforts, the authorities adopt a new policy. The bodies are cremated where they lie in subterranean caverns. The soldiers use flamethrowers to carry out this grim task.

During the course of the excavations, while the men are still under German command, Edgar Derby is discovered with a teapot found in the ruins. He is arrested and convicted of plundering, then executed by firing squad.

Soon it is spring, and the Germans disappear to fight or flee the Russians. The war ends. Trees sprout leaves. Billy finds the horses and the green, coffin-shaped wagon. A bird says to him, "*Poo-tee-weet?*"

ANALYSIS

The bird asks a question, "*Poo-tee-weet?*" to which there can be no reply. As the narrator warns in the first chapter, there is nothing intelligent to say about a massacre. The novel's ending suggests that bird-talk makes as much sense as anyone's talk about war. Yet, like the bird, Vonnegut has persisted in filling the silence left after the massacre. Even if words and stories are meaningless, that they have managed to survive at all in the aftermath of a war that saw the mass incineration of books as well as of bodies is quite a feat. Moreover, Vonnegut has succeeded in constructing a thing of beauty out of the shards of senselessness and anguish.

In the end, the problem of dignity returns. Every one of the hundreds of thousands of people born every day wants dignity. The equalizing power of death brings dignity at a high price. Billy must travel far from this planet to find his own sort of dignity. Vonnegut wonders if there will ever be enough dignity to go around here on earth. There is no answer to this question, either.

In *Slaughterhouse-Five* Vonnegut not only dismisses conventional story structure, which includes a climax, but he also shows how the war has made the idea of a climax completely irrelevant. While Vonnegut suggests to O'Hare early in the novel that the story should climax in the shooting of Edgar Derby for plundering a teapot, his portrayal of this moment is quite matter-of-fact: "Somewhere in there the poor old high school teacher, Edgar Derby, was caught with a teapot he had taken from the catacombs. He was arrested for plundering. He was tried and shot. So it goes." In another narrative, the death of such a kind, just man might be the ultimate tragic irony. But with the phrase, "So it goes," Vonnegut implies that there is no justice in death.

The Tralfamadorians advise eternally revisiting the pleasant moments of one's life, but Billy Pilgrim exerts no control over his time-traveling. Likewise, we often lack control over our own memories, which may make it hard for us to find comforting Billy's message about the eternity of moments. Furthermore, a Tralfamadorian universe implies more accountability than Billy would have us believe, for if a pleasant moment lasts forever, so does an awful one like the firebombing of Dresden. Those responsible continually relive the direct consequences of their decision. Somewhere, Billy Pilgrim's moment of sheer joy dozing in the spring sunshine still exists. But somewhere else, 130,000 civilians are burning and suffocating. Still elsewhere, prisoners of war will eternally uncover an infinite mine of corpses. Time cannot erase such moments.

Important Quotations Explained

1. *It is so short and jumbled and jangled, Sam, because there is nothing intelligent to say about a massacre. Everybody is supposed to be dead, to never say anything or want anything ever again. Everything is supposed to be very quiet after a massacre, and it always is, except for the birds. And what do the birds say? All there is to say about a massacre, things like "Poo-tee-weet?"*

Kurt Vonnegut, as the narrator, addresses his publisher Seymour ("Sam") Lawrence directly in this passage from Chapter 1. He seems to apologize for delivering such a short, fragmented manuscript. The irony of this passage is that if there is nothing intelligent to say about a massacre, then writing a book about one, no matter how short, is a major accomplishment. Perhaps like birdsong, the book merely serves as a simple communication demonstrating that life still exists in a devastated world. The bird's inquisitive refrain returns in the very last line of the novel, leaving us with the unanswered question of what life is like in the aftermath of war—life's most devastating enemy.

2.   *Billy had a framed prayer on his office wall which expressed*
     his method for keeping going, even though he was
     unenthusiastic about living. A lot of patients who saw the
     prayer on Billy's wall told him that it helped them to keep
     going, too. It went like this: "God grant me the serenity to
     accept the things I cannot change, courage to change the
     things I can, and wisdom always to tell the difference."
     Among the things Billy Pilgrim could not change were the
     past, the present, and the future.

This passage occurs in Chapter 3, after Billy has been kidnapped
and taken to Tralfamadore in 1968. There he sees the same inscription on a locket around the neck of Montana Wildhack, the actress
brought to mate with Billy in the Tralfamadorian zoo. The saying
brings to light the central conflict of Billy's attempt to live a Tralfamadorian life in a human world: he subscribes to the Tralfamadorian belief that there is a fourth dimension of time and that time is
cyclical, but he lives in a world in which everyone believes that time
moves in a single, linear progression. Tralfamadorians would argue
that humans never know the difference between the things they cannot change because there is no difference; nothing is negotiable in a
universe of predefined, structured moments.

QUOTATIONS

3. *Billy answered. There was a drunk on the other end. Billy could almost smell his breath—mustard gas and roses. It was a wrong number. Billy hung up.*

In Chapter 4, the night after his daughter's wedding in 1967, Billy gets up out of bed, unable to sleep. He knows that the flying saucer will come for him soon. He wanders into his daughter's empty bedroom, the phone rings, and on the other end is a drunk. It is unusual that Billy claims he can almost to smell the mustard gas and roses on his breath over the phone. This detail emerges through a kind of empathy that seems to connect otherwise unrelated moments in the omniscient narration. We, the readers, recognize this drunk from Chapter 1: he is the author, Kurt Vonnegut, who in his middle age has a tendency to make drunken phone calls late at night to old girl-friends, his breath stinking of mustard gas and roses. The odd combination of mustard gas, often used as a chemical weapon, and roses, a symbol of romance, highlights how deeply the war has affected Vonnegut's life.

4. *"If I hadn't spent so much time studying Earthlings,"* said
the Tralfamadorian, *"I wouldn't have any idea what was
meant by 'free will.' I've visited thirty-one inhabited planets
in the universe, and I have studied reports on one hundred
more. Only on Earth is there any talk of free will."*

This quotation comes at the end of Chapter 4, as Billy listens to his captors describe the true nature of time. These words reveal that not only do Tralfamadorians have a completely deterministic view of the universe in which every moment is structured beyond the control of its participants, but that they also lack an awareness of the possibility of free will. The alien who talks to Billy is an exception, having encountered the peculiarly human hang-up in his travels. But he maintains that humans, alone among all beings in the universe, believe in the illusion of free will. His emphasis on the idea of "studying" humans and inhabitants of other planets makes humans (and their conception of free will) and other non-Tralfamadorians seem like bizarre exceptions to the rule of nature. He thus performs a reversal of the human tendency to think of alien life as abnormal.

5. *There isn't any particular relationship between the
    messages, except that the author has chosen them carefully,
    so that, when seen all at once, they produce an image of life
    that is beautiful and surprising and deep. There is no
    beginning, no middle, no end, no suspense, no moral, no
    causes, no effects. What we love in our books are the depths
    of many marvelous moments seen all at one time.*

In this passage at the beginning of Chapter 5, one of Billy's captors
explains the Tralfamadorian novel to him. It seems that Vonnegut
has taken this template as a model for *Slaughterhouse-Five,* down to
the rows of asterisks or dots separating short clumps of text. The
irony of such a strategy is that Vonnegut, like Billy, lacks the Tralfamadorian ability to pick and choose his moments. Vonnegut thus
considers his book a failure of sorts, because he has achieved the
Tralfamadorian structure without its accompanying depth and
beauty, and because he has come up with nothing more intelligent or
deep to say about a massacre than *"Poo-tee-weet."* Most readers
would argue, however, that Vonnegut has actually succeeded in
making a thing of great beauty out of a collection of tragic moments.

QUOTATIONS

KEY FACTS

FULL TITLE
Slaughterhouse-Five; or, The Children's Crusade: A Duty-Dance with Death

AUTHOR
Kurt Vonnegut

TYPE OF WORK
Novel

GENRE
Antiwar novel; historical fiction; science fiction; semi-autobiographical fiction

LANGUAGE
English

TIME AND PLACE WRITTEN
Approximately 1945–1968, United States

DATE OF FIRST PUBLICATION
1969

PUBLISHER
Dell Publishing

NARRATOR
The author; or arguably, sometimes an anonymous narrator with a similar point of view

POINT OF VIEW
The author narrates in both first and third person. The first-person sections are confined mainly to the first and last chapters. The narration is omniscient: it reveals the thoughts and motives of several characters, and provides details about their lives and some analysis of their motivations. The narrator primarily follows Billy Pilgrim but also presents the point of view of other characters whom Billy encounters.

TONE
The narrator's tone is familiar and ironic, and he uncovers touches of dark humor and absurdity that do not diminish the

lyrical and emotional power of the material. His portrayal of Billy is intimate but ambivalent, and he occasionally emphasizes the diction of reported speech (prefacing a passage with "He says that" or "Billy says") to draw a distinction between reality and Billy's interpretation of events.

TENSE

The majority of the book is written in the past tense, but the narrator occasionally uses the present tense—especially in the first and last chapters—when speaking from a personal point of view as Kurt Vonnegut. The reporting of Billy's speech is in the present tense (for example: "Billy Pilgrim has come unstuck in time. Or so he says.") Occasionally the tense switches to future, as when Billy describes his future death.

SETTING (TIME)

The narrative provides a detailed account of Billy's war experiences in 1944–1945, but it skips around his entire life, from his early childhood in the 1920s to his death in 1976. The author's narration is set in 1968.

SETTING (PLACE)

The narrative thread of 1944–1945 concerns Billy's army service in Germany and briefly in Luxembourg, where he is captured after the Battle of the Bulge. Most of the rest of Billy's life takes place in Ilium, New York. He also travels to the planet Tralfamadore and lives there in a zoo.

PROTAGONIST

Billy Pilgrim

MAJOR CONFLICT

Billy struggles to make sense out of a life forever marked by the firsthand experience of war's tragedy.

RISING ACTION

Billy and his fellow prisoners are transported across Germany and begin living in a slaughterhouse prison and working in the city of Dresden.

CLIMAX

Dresden is incinerated in a deadly firebomb attack. But Billy misses the moment of destruction, waiting out the attack in a well-protected meat locker. Psychologically, Billy does not come to terms with this event until nearly twenty years later, when the sight of a barbershop quartet on his wedding anniversary triggers his suppressed sense of grief.

FALLING ACTION

The falling action occurs in the realm of Billy's later life as he progresses toward a newfound consciousness and an increasingly tenuous mental state. Billy experiences alien abduction and prepares to share his new insights with the world.

THEMES

The destructiveness of war; the illusion of free will; the importance of sight

MOTIFS

"So it goes"; the presence of the narrator as a character

SYMBOLS

The bird who says "*Poo-tee-weet?*"; the colors blue and ivory

FORESHADOWING

The narrative convention that Vonnegut dispenses with most thoroughly in this book is foreshadowing. He outlines all the events of Billy's life before proceeding with the story.

STUDY QUESTIONS & ESSAY TOPICS

STUDY QUESTIONS

1.   What is the relationship between the structure and the content of SLAUGHTERHOUSE-FIVE?

The novel's random, skipping timeline presents an effective method of representing one man's inability to live a normal life after experiencing modern warfare. The disjointed collage of Billy Pilgrim's life gets translated directly to the disjointed collage of the narrative. We experience Billy's life as he does, without suspense or logical order, randomly orbiting about the firebombing of Dresden.

A traditional novel might start with a youthful Billy Pilgrim and follow him into old age or with an elderly protagonist who flashes back on his life. Billy, however, adopts a Tralfamadorian attitude because it is the only way he can make sense of the loose grip on time he is left with after the war. In order to follow him, the narrative approximates the same attitude. A Tralfamadorian novel, as discussed in Chapter 5, contains urgent, discrete messages describing scenes and situations. The author of such a novel carefully chooses the messages so that, when seen all at once, they form a profound image of life. Otherwise, there is no obvious relationship among them—there is no beginning, middle, climax, or end.

Humans, of course, cannot perceive all the elements of a novel at the same time. We can only approximate this effect like we approximate motion on film—with quick snapshots shown in rapid succession. Showing the snapshots in chronological order yields a traditional linear narrative; shuffling them up yields the closest approximation of a Tralfamadorian whole. Vonnegut entrusts his long-in-the-making Dresden book to a Tralfamadorian template in the hopes that it will produce something profound and beautiful from the memories of a massacre.

2. *Briefly discuss some of the consequences of a Tralfamadorian view of the universe for a human.*

The Tralfamadorians see all of time simultaneously. They know what has happened and what will happen and are able to focus on the nice moments. Things always happen the way they do because of how moments are structured, and no one can do anything to change the future. In fact, the concept of change is difficult for a Tralfamadorian to grasp. To them, free will is just a bizarre fiction discussed on Earth, where people cannot see in four dimensions. All time is fixed, but each moment is always accessible to Tralfamadorians, so they can pick and choose what they want to experience. Each moment essentially exists forever.

Without free will, there seems to be no accountability. There is also no time wasted in blame and punishment. Billy does not blame anyone for what he sees in Dresden, for what he experiences in the war, or for the death of his wife. He simply accepts that things happen as they happen.

There also seems to be no incentive to live one's life well (according to whatever definition one might have of living well). As long as every life has a few good moments, the time traveler can eternally visit those and be eternally content. However, judging from Billy's experiences, humans do not seem as able to control time travel or remember with the same selectivity as Tralfamadorians. Billy has no say in his comings and goings through time. Thus, he relives atrocity and horror as much as he relives moments of happiness. If atrocities also last forever to be eternally relived, perhaps there is incentive not to act atrociously after all.

3. *How does Vonnegut's technique of time-shifting affect*
    our understanding of the novel? Is there an advantage
    to structuring SLAUGHTERHOUSE-FIVE *in the*
    "telegraphic schizophrenic manner"? If not, is it too
    random to allow a cohesive, linear story to emerge?

A linear story does emerge out of the jumble of time-shifted details in the novel: the story of Billy Pilgrim, POW, making his way through time and across the European theater of World War II toward Dresden, the scene of ultimate destruction. Every time we return to this thread of the narrative, it unfolds in chronological order. Interspersed in this order are wild zigzags forward and backward through Billy's life. These time jumps might be confusing, but they give force to the horror we encounter along the way. Vonnegut feeds the novel's emotional momentum with the transitions between time jumps. For example, in Chapter 3 Billy is transported from his bed in Ilium, where he weeps after seeing cripples in the street, to the POW march in Luxembourg, where he weeps because of the wind in his eyes. Such transitions take the place of traditional narrative devices such as foreshadowing. Vonnegut gives away the climax he had been considering for his grand narrative (Edgar Derby's execution) in Chapter 1; when we finally get to the telling of it, at the end of Chapter 10, it comes as an afterthought.

In addition, the novel might be schizophrenic, but it is not random. On the one hand, death strikes indiscriminately, and we never know who the next victim will be. But, on the other hand, the sheer volume of seemingly random deaths adds up to an emotional weight like that of the Tralfamadorian novel described in Chapter 5.

Suggested Essay Topics

1. Many Vonnegut novels deal with traffickers of "useful lies." Are the lessons of Tralfamadore useful lies? Why or why not?

2. Is Billy Pilgrim sane or insane? Does it matter?

3. Discuss the use of irony or black humor in Slaughterhouse-Five.

4. What does Vonnegut achieve by placing himself as a character in the story?

Review & Resources

Quiz

1. What do the Tralfamadorians resemble?

   A. Windshield wipers
   B. Toilet plungers
   C. Humans
   D. Golliwogs

2. Where is Billy Pilgrim from?

   A. Ilium, New York
   B. Ithaca, New York
   C. New York, New York
   D. Schenectady, New York

3. Of how many dimensions are Tralfamadorians aware?

   A. One
   B. Two
   C. Three
   D. Four

4. Who lends Billy his science-fiction books?

   A. Eliot Rosewater
   B. Howard J. Campbell, Jr.
   C. Bertram Copeland Rumfoord
   D. Kilgore Trout

5. To whom does Vonnegut make the promise that he will call his book The Children's Crusade?

   A. Bertram Copeland Rumfoord
   B. Lily Rumfoord
   C. Mary O'Hare
   D. Gerhard Müller

6. Following which event is Billy taken prisoner?

    A.   The bombing of Dresden
    B.   The Battle of the Bulge
    C.   The Children's Crusade
    D.   The Battle of Kursk

7. Why do the Tralfamadorians compare Billy to a bug trapped in amber?

    A.   Because Billy is skinny like a bug
    B.   Because Billy is trapped on Tralfamadore
    C.   Because Billy has no control over his fate
    D.   Because Billy's mother's birthstone is amber

8. Whom should one ask for when one is in Cody, Wyoming, according to the novel?

    A.   Wild Bill Hickock
    B.   Wild Bob
    C.   Captain Safety
    D.   Buffalo Bill Cody

9. In what city does Kurt Vonnegut work for General Electric?

    A.   Indianapolis, Indiana
    B.   Chicago, Illinois
    C.   Iowa City, Iowa
    D.   Schenectady, New York

10. How many children does Billy father?

    A.   One
    B.   Two
    C.   Three
    D.   Four

11. Which of the following is the title of a Kilgore Trout novel?

    A.   *The Big Board*
    B.   *Bluebeard*
    C.   *The Clever Man and the Cutout*
    D.   *Everything Was Beautiful, and Nothing Hurt*

12. What single event in the war makes Billy cry?

    A.   The death of Roland Weary
    B.   Tasting a spoonful of malt syrup
    C.   The sight of crippled men walking with crutches
    D.   The condition of the horses that pull the green wagon

13. In what year does Billy die?

    A.   1967
    B.   1968
    C.   1970
    D.   1976

14. Where do Billy and Valencia go on their honeymoon?

    A.   Cape Cod, Massachusetts
    B.   Cape Ann, Massachusetts
    C.   Sugarbush Mountain, Vermont
    D.   Niagara Falls

15. Where does the author show up at the POW camp?

    A.   In the latrine
    B.   In the hospital
    C.   In the production of *Cinderella*
    D.   In the shower room

16. What is Edgar Derby tried and executed for stealing?

    A.   A diamond
    B.   A clock in the shape of the Eiffel Tower
    C.   A teapot
    D.   A denture

17. Which of the following happens to Billy for the first time in Dresden?

    A.   He gets kidnapped by aliens
    B.   He comes unstuck in time
    C.   He sees a naked woman
    D.   He feels "animal magnetism"

REVIEW & RESOURCES

18. Why did Valencia think that no one would marry her?

    A. Because her father is an optometrist
    B. Because she is shy
    C. Because all the eligible men were away at war
    D. Because she is fat

19. What does Billy's doctor prescribe to help him sleep?

    A. Shock therapy
    B. A Magic Fingers vibrator
    C. Sleeping pills
    D. A vacation to Vermont

20. Why is it ironic that the Serenity Prayer hangs in Billy's office?

    A. Because he is skeptical of religion and views the prayer as a farce
    B. Because he recovered it from the ashes of Dresden
    C. Because it suggests the possibility of improving the world, which Billy believes impossible
    D. Because it is a prayer for deliverance from evil, a concept that the novel undermines

21. How does Bertram Copeland Rumfoord respond to Billy's claim that he was in Dresden at the time of the firebombing?

    A. He calls Billy a liar
    B. He asks Billy for proof
    C. He tries to change the subject
    D. He asks to interview Billy for the book he's writing

22. What is inscribed in Montana Wildhack's silver locket?

    A. The Serenity Prayer
    B. The Lord's Prayer
    C. "Billy Pilgrim"
    D. "Tralfamadore"

23. In what format are Tralfamadorian books composed?

    A.   They are all composed on tape in audio format

    B.   They are all composed in small booklike computers that can change at will

    C.   They are composed of short telegram-like groups of symbols separated by stars

    D.   None. Tralfmadorians don't read books

24. On which U.S. city does Billy say China will drop a hydrogen bomb in 1976?

    A.   New York City

    B.   Chicago

    C.   Los Angeles

    D.   Washington, D.C.

25. What question does Billy ask the aliens when he is abducted?

    A.   "Where are we going?"

    B.   "What is the meaning of life?"

    C.   "How does the world end?"

    D.   "Why me?"

REVIEW & RESOURCES

ANSWER KEY:
1: B; 2: A; 3: D; 4: A; 5: C; 6: B; 7: C; 8: B; 9: D; 10: B; 11: A;
12: D; 13: D; 14: B; 15: B; 16: C; 17: C; 18: D; 19: D; 20: C;
21: C; 22: A; 23: C; 24: C; 25: D;

SUGGESTIONS FOR FURTHER READING

ALLEN, WILLIAM RODNEY. *Understanding Kurt Vonnegut.*
Columbia: University of South Carolina Press, 1991.

KLINKOWITZ, JEROME, and JOHN SOMER, eds. *The Vonnegut Statement.* New York: Delacorte, 1973.

LUNDQUIST, JAMES. *Kurt Vonnegut.* New York: Frederick Ungar Publishing, 1977.

MUSTAZZA, LEONARD, ed. *The Critical Response to Kurt Vonnegut.* Westport, Connecticut: Greenwood Press, 1994.

SIEPMANN, KATHERINE BAKER, ed. *Benet's Reader's Encyclopedia.* New York: HarperCollins, 1987.

VONNEGUT, KURT, JR. *Palm Sunday.* New York: Delacorte Press, 1981.

———. *Wampeters, Foma, & Granfalloons.* New York: Delacorte Press, 1992.

REVIEW & RESOURCES

SPARKNOTES
TEST PREPARATION
GUIDES

The SparkNotes team figured it was time to cut standardized tests down to size. We've studied the tests for you, so that SparkNotes test prep guides are:

Smarter:
Packed with critical-thinking skills and test-
taking strategies that will improve your score.

Better:
Fully up to date, covering all new features of the tests,
with study tips on every type of question.

Faster:
Our books cover exactly what you need to
know for the test. No more, no less.

SPARKNOTES™ LITERATURE GUIDES